THE DESIGNS OF
WILLIAM MORRIS

THE DESIGNS OF
WILLIAM MORRIS

WATERCOLOUR DESIGN FOR **VINE** WALLPAPER, 1874

William Morris's importance as a design revolutionary cannot be over-emphasized. A man of prodigious energy and manifold talents, he was responsible for drawing public attention away from the dull commercialization imposed by the Industrial Revolution and leading it back towards the fresh and simple traditions of handcrafted medieval design. A romantic idealist who drew much of his inspiration from nature, Morris's golden rule was 'Have nothing in your houses which you do not know to be useful or believe to be beautiful'.

During the course of a career which spanned just 40 years, Morris produced a huge array of designs and patterns. They were seen on stained glass, wallpapers, carpets, tapestries, printed textiles and a range of small items. This book presents just a selection, taken not only from the output of Morris himself but also from that of his companies, Morris, Marshall, Faulkner & Co. and Morris and Co. All of them show Morris's 'heaven-sent gift' to create successful and original designs whose appeal is as irresistible today as it was a century ago.

TRELLIS WALLPAPER, 1864
WATERCOLOUR DESIGN FOR **TRELLIS** WALLPAPER, 1864

LARKSPUR WALLPAPER, 1872 (OVERLEAF)

ORNAMENTAL LETTER
PEACOCK AND DRAGON WOVEN WOOL FABRIC, 1878

BLUE POMEGRANATE WALLPAPER, 1866 (OVERLEAF)

ST JAMES'S CEILING WALLPAPER, 1881
PORTIÈRE, c. 1890

AFRICAN MARIGOLD PRINTED COTTON, 1876
KENNET WOVEN SILK, 1883

CABBAGE AND VINE TAPESTRY, 1879 (OVERLEAF)

WATERCOLOUR DESIGN FOR **AFRICAN MARIGOLD** PRINTED COTTON, 1876

BACHELOR'S BUTTON WALLPAPER, 1892

POWDERED PRINTED COTTON, c. 1902 (OVERLEAF)

KENNET PRINTED COTTON, 1883
BIRD AND ANEMONE PRINTED COTTON, 1882

EVENLODE PRINTED COTTON, 1883 (OVERLEAF)

WATERCOLOUR DESIGN FOR **THE ORCHARD** TAPESTRY, c. 1890

THE ORCHARD TAPESTRY, 1890

APPLE WALLPAPER, 1877 (OVERLEAF)

BRUGES WALLPAPER, 1888
WATERCOLOUR DESIGN FOR **WREATH** WOVEN CARPET, c. 1876

SEAWEED WALLPAPER, 1901 (OVERLEAF)

WATERCOLOUR DESIGN FOR **QUATREFOIL** RUG, c. 1890
ROSE WALLPAPER, 1877

EMBROIDERED CUSHION COVER, c. 1876
TREE PORTIÈRE TAPESTRY, c. 1909

ACORN EMBOSSED OR STAMPED SILK VELVET, c. 1900 (OVERLEAF)

JASMINE WALLPAPER, 1872
HAMMERSMITH WOOL RUG, c. 1880

WREATH WALLPAPER, 1876 (OVERLEAF)

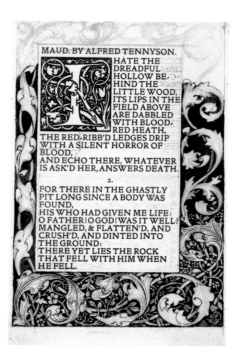

MAUD. BY ALFRED TENNYSON.

I HATE THE DREADFUL HOLLOW BEHIND THE LITTLE WOOD, ITS LIPS IN THE FIELD ABOVE ARE DABBLED WITH BLOOD-RED HEATH, THE RED-RIBB'D LEDGES DRIP WITH A SILENT HORROR OF BLOOD, AND ECHO THERE, WHATEVER IS ASK'D HER, ANSWERS DEATH.

2.

FOR THERE IN THE GHASTLY PIT LONG SINCE A BODY WAS FOUND, HIS WHO HAD GIVEN ME LIFE: O FATHER! O GOD! WAS IT WELL? MANGLED, & FLATTEN'D, AND CRUSH'D, AND DINTED INTO THE GROUND: THERE YET LIES THE ROCK THAT FELL WITH HIM WHEN HE FELL.

PEN AND INK DESIGN FOR TENNYSON'S 'MAUD', 1893

ORNAMENTAL LETTERS

WATERCOLOUR DESIGN FOR **CHRYSANTHEMUM** WALLPAPER, 1877 (OVERLEAF)

STAINED-GLASS WINDOW, 1878
BULLERSWOOD CARPET, c. 1889

LARKSPUR PRINTED SILK, 1875 (OVERLEAF)

TILE PANEL, 1876
'16 SQUARE' TILE, 1870

BROCATEL WOVEN WOOL FABRIC, c. 1888 (OVERLEAF)

WATERCOLOUR DESIGN FOR **ACANTHUS** WALLPAPER, 1875
ACANTHUS WALLPAPER, 1875

GARDEN TULIP WALLPAPER, c. 1885
VIOLET AND COLUMBINE WOVEN FABRIC, 1883

CRAY PRINTED COTTON, 1884 (OVERLEAF)

DAFFODIL PRINTED COTTON, c. 1891
FLOWERPOT EMBROIDERED CUSHION COVER, 1880

UTRECHT VELVET EMBOSSED MOHAIR PLUSH, c. 1871 (OVERLEAF)

PIMPERNEL WALLPAPER, 1876
WATERCOLOUR DESIGN FOR **AVON** CHINTZ, c. 1887

WALLFLOWER WALLPAPER, c. 1890 (OVERLEAF)

TILE PORTRAYING ROSSETTI AS CHAUCER, 1864

CARPET, 1890s

BROTHER RABBIT PRINTED COTTON, 1882

WATERCOLOUR AND INK DESIGN FOR ORNAMENTAL LETTER

BOWER WALLPAPER, 1877 (OVERLEAF)

GRAFTON WALLPAPER, 1883
MINSTREL ANGEL WITH DULCIMER STAINED-GLASS WINDOW, 1882

BIRD WOVEN WOOL FABRIC, 1878 (OVERLEAF)

HAMMERSMITH RUG, c. 1890

ORNAMENTAL LETTER

EDEN PRINTED COTTON, c. 1905 (OVERLEAF)

PRAISE OF VENUS

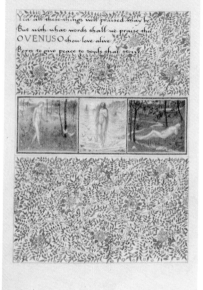

Yea all these things will praised may be
But with what words shall we praise thee
O VENUS O thou love alive
Born to give peace to souls that strive

PAGE FROM *A BOOK OF VERSE*, 1870

DESIGN FOR EMBROIDERY, c. 1875

LODDEN PRINTED COTTON, 1884 (OVERLEAF)

CARTOON FOR **THE PELICAN** STAINED-GLASS
WINDOW, 1880
WILLOW BOUGHS WALLPAPER, 1887

PAGE FROM CHAUCER, 1896
MARIGOLD PRINTED COTTON, 1875

FRITILLARY WALLPAPER, 1885 (OVERLEAF)

WOODPECKER TAPESTRY, 1885
WATERCOLOUR DESIGN FOR **ROSE AND THISTLE** PRINTED COTTON, 1881

ARTICHOKE EMBROIDERED HANGING, 1876 (OVERLEAF)

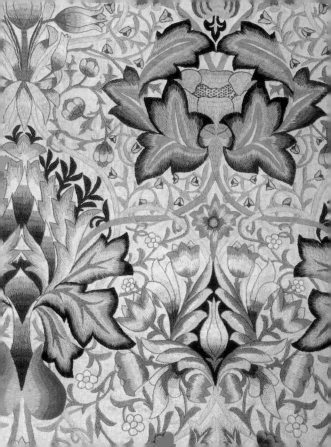

EMBROIDERED HANGING, c. 1880
WATERCOLOUR DESIGN FOR EMBROIDERY, 1870s

WANDLE PRINTED COTTON, 1884 (OVERLEAF)

DESIGNS FOR ORNAMENTAL LETTERS

ORNAMENTAL LETTER

THE STRAWBERRY THIEF PRINTED COTTON, 1883 (OVERLEAF)

SUNFLOWER WALLPAPER, 1879
NORWICH WALLPAPER, c. 1889

TULIP AND ROSE WOVEN FABRIC, 1876 (OVERLEAF)

MEDWAY PRINTED COTTON, 1885
WATERCOLOUR DESIGN FOR STAINED-GLASS WINDOW, 1876

FLOWER GARDEN WOVEN SILK, 1879 (OVERLEAF)

WATERCOLOUR DESIGN FOR **REDCAR** CARPET, c. 1885
LOTUS EMBROIDERED HANGING, 1880s

WINDRUSH PRINTED COTTON, 1883 (OVERLEAF)

WATERCOLOUR DESIGN FOR COTTON DAMASK, c. 1876

WATERCOLOUR DESIGN FOR **CABBAGE AND VINE** TAPESTRY, 1879

ROSE PRINTED COTTON, 1883
ORNAMENTAL LETTER

ST MARY MAGDALENE AND ST JOHN THE EVANGELIST
STAINED-GLASS WINDOW, 1865

ST PETER STAINED-GLASS WINDOW, 1876

WATERCOLOUR DESIGN FOR **EVENLODE** PRINTED COTTON, 1883
ISPAHAN WOVEN WOOL FABRIC, c. 1888

DAISY TILES, 1862 (OVERLEAF)

'ANGELI LAUDANTES' TAPESTRY, 1894
DOVE AND ROSE WOOL AND SILK FABRIC, 1879

HONEYSUCKLE WALLPAPER, 1883 (OVERLEAF)

ORNAMENTAL LETTERS
HORNPOPPY WALLPAPER, 1880s

WEY PRINTED COTTON, c. 1883
DAISY WALLPAPER, 1862

BLACKTHORN WALLPAPER, 1892 (OVERLEAF)

WATERCOLOUR DESIGN FOR EMBROIDERY, 1870s
TULIP AND LILY CARPET, c. 1875

WILD TULIP WALLPAPER, 1884 (OVERLEAF)

ANEMONE WALLPAPER, 1890s
ORNAMENTAL LETTERS

SINGLE STEM WALLPAPER, 1890s (OVERLEAF)

Born on 24 March 1834 at Elm House, Walthamstow, William Morris was the son of a successful City broker who brought his nine children up in an atmosphere of contented middle-class opulence. In 1848, the year after his father's death, Morris was sent away to school at Marlborough College where he was remembered as the boy who spent his days making nets in which to capture birds and fish. This early interest in nature was further developed at Oxford, whither Morris went in 1853 to read Theology at Exeter College. Here he quickly found himself at the centre of a group of spirited and artistic students, amongst them Edward Burne-Jones (1833-98) who shared many of Morris's enthusiasms and was to remain a lifelong friend. It was amid the romantic buildings and medieval architecture of Oxford that Morris intensified his passion for all things medieval and formed strong views on the importance of art and handcraftsmanship. In fact his views grew to be so strong that he decided to give up his intended career as a clergyman and turn instead to architecture and a life of design.

In 1856 Morris entered the offices of GE Street, the Gothic Revival architect who was later to make his name as the designer of the Law Courts in London. His time there was brief but significant, for it was in Street's office that he met the architect Philip Webb (1831-1915) and, encouraged by his friends, determined to try his hand as an artist. He moved into an apartment in Red Lion Square, London, with Burne-Jones, who was also keen to launch himself upon a career as a painter. One of their first commissions was the decoration of the new Oxford Union debating hall, a job which was undertaken with Dante Gabriel Rossetti (1828-82) amongst others. A group endeavour, all those involved enjoyed themselves immensely and the resulting murals glow with an enthusiastic vibrancy. For Morris this was a particularly significant task since one of the models was the eighteen-year-old Jane Burden, the 'Stunner', with whom he fell instantly in love.

The wedding, which took place in Oxford in 1859, was a relatively quiet affair. Afterwards Morris and Jane settled down together at the

Red House at Bexleyheath in Kent, a house which was designed by Philip Webb and furnished throughout by Morris and his friends. Decorated in the medieval style, it represented an instant antidote to the fussy formalism of the Victorian era with its simple materials and air of calm beauty and it quickly became a pivotal centre for the Morris circle. Here they would meet at weekends, planning future design schemes and discussing their visions of an ideal world. And it must have been at the Red House that the original idea for the design firm of Morris, Marshall, Faulkner & Co was first mooted and then formalized.

A collaboration of 7 friends (Morris, Burne-Jones, Webb, Rossetti, Ford Madox Brown, Charles Faulkner and Peter Paul Marshall), the firm was founded in 1861 and was able to exhibit furniture, stained glass and embroideries in the Medieval Court of the 1862 Great Exhibition. Morris, Marshall, Faulkner & Co won 2 medals at the Exhibition and a number of important commissions, including the Green Dining Room at the South Kensington Museum, resulted. Within a relatively short time and due largely to the efficiency and imagination of its business managers, as well as to the charm of the designs, the firm had won the support of prominent architects and other discerning patrons and it was able to build on this success and move steadily forward. Concentrating initially on stained-glass designs, it soon began to include wallpapers and then printed textiles. In every case Morris chose the design to suit the medium and to make the best of its potential. His skill lay in his understanding of different textures and materials and his insistence on choosing the right design. Morris's designs are characterized by a new vividness and feel for nature, providing a stark contrast to the flat formalism of Owen Jones and the lurid vulgarity of the 1850s.

Unfortunately life at the Red House had not proved sustainable, largely due to Morris's ill health. The Morrises now had 2 daughters, Jenny (1861-1935) and May (1862-1938), and found that travelling to and from London was not practical. In 1865 they installed themselves at 26 Queen Square and then, in 1871, took a tenancy of Kelmscott Manor at Lechlade in

Gloucestershire. The perfect country retreat, unfortunately Kelmscott did not turn out to be the idyllically happy family home it should have been. The cracks which had been gradually developing in the Morrises' marriage over Janey's attachment to Rossetti could no longer be ignored, especially since Rossetti was now a joint tenant. It was during this period that Morris undertook two long journeys to Iceland, furthering his interest in the language and mythology of this mystical land. When his personal life grew too difficult, he could always find solace in some new and all-absorbing enthusiasm.

Yet by 1874 Rossetti's affair with Janey was over. Ever since his wife's suicide in 1862, Rossetti had become increasingly unbalanced and difficult to deal with until Janey had finally decided that the relationship could continue no longer. Rossetti moved out and Morris found that he could then start to find pleasure in Kelmscott itself. It was to remain his country home and the source of some of his greatest joy until his death.

Over the years Morris had come to realize that the structure of the firm had changed and that the responsibility for its organization lay mainly in his hands. Thus in 1875 the old partnership was dissolved and Morris & Co was set up. This was also the year in which Morris's interest in textile design began. It was furthered through a long working partnership with the silk and cotton chintz dyer Thomas Wardle at Leek in Staffordshire. Both men were aiming to experiment with old recipes and techniques and to use natural dyes to produce the bright, primary colours Morris loved. Never happier than when absorbed in work, Morris found these experiments fascinating and in the mid-1870s he also began to find out more about weaving and carpet design, inspired by an interest in Eastern patterns. Over half of a total of forty beautiful chintz designs, for which he is best known, date from this period.

In 1877 Morris & Co opened showrooms on Oxford Street, thus establishing themselves in the public eye as a company of note. It soon became a fashion imperative for all artistically-aware Londoners to own at least one item of Morris manufacture and many style-conscious families commissioned the firm to carry out the entire decoration and furnishing of their houses. In fact the business was expanding so rapidly that in 1881 it became necessary to find alternative workshop space. The site chosen was at Merton Abbey in Surrey on the banks of the River Wardle. Charmingly rural, it was an inspirational setting and here Morris was to produce some of his finest work and to explore further his interest in textiles and particularly in carpet-weaving and tapestries. His daughter May was herself a talented embroiderer and designer who took over this section of the business from 1885.

Yet it was not only as a designer that Morris was to find fame in his own lifetime. He was also a writer of visionary, romantic verse who was offered (but declined) the Poet Laureateship on Tennyson's death. His first volume of poetry, *The Defence of Guenevere*, appeared in 1858 and this was followed by *The Earthly Paradise*, an epic cycle of narrative poems produced during the 1860s. One of the first to translate the Icelandic sagas, much of his poetry concentrated on retelling the classical myths and medieval tales which held so much fascination for him.

His trips to Iceland fuelled this enthusiasm and gave him a lifelong passion for the raw beauty and long tradition of the country.

In 1883, after some years of being interested in socialism, Morris joined the Democratic Federation and became a key figure in the socialist movement, involving himself in public debates and lectures and throwing himself into a cause which he had long believed to be just and right. Considering himself to be a communist, one of his chief aims was to further the cause of revolutionary socialism. He tried to ensure that his workshops were run along democratic lines and that the employees worked in decent conditions and were paid above-average wages. *News from Nowhere*, his great Utopian novel, was published in 1890 and assured Morris's reputation as an active socialist.

During the last years of his life Morris turned his attention to the art and craft of printing and in 1891 he founded the Kelmscott Press in Hammersmith and printed a total of over 50 titles, including Ruskin's 'On the Nature of Gothic' from *The Stones of Venice*. The Press occupied him for his last 5 years but it soon became clear that his health was failing and that he was not likely to live much longer. As Morris lay dying in October 1896, one of his doctors pronounced his disease as 'simply being William Morris'. A man of unbounded energy and endless enthusiasm, he was unable to do anything halfheartedly and in a relatively short lifetime did 'more work than most ten men'. Scruffy in appearance with a huge bushy beard, his straightforward manner and willingness to work alongside his employees lent his workshops an air of well-being and contentment. Morris's pervasive influence and multi-faceted personality ensured that his place as a key figure in nineteenth-century design can never be forgotten.

PICTURE ACKNOWLEDGEMENTS

All designs are by Morris, unless otherwise stated.

BAL
Bridgeman Art Library, London

V&A
Victoria and Albert Museum, London

WMG
William Morris Gallery (London Borough of Waltham Forest)

Iris wallpaper, 1890s. Designed by JH Dearle. BAL/V&A.

Two details from **Forest** tapestry, 1887. Designed by Morris and JH Dearle, the animals in this tapestry were drawn by Philip Webb. V&A.

Watercolour design for **Vine** wallpaper, 1874. V&A.

Trellis wallpaper, 1864. BAL/V&A.

Watercolour design for **Trellis** wallpaper, 1864. WMG.

Larkspur wallpaper, 1872. V&A.

Ornamental letter designed for the Kelmscott Press, 1890s. WMG.

Peacock and Dragon woven wool fabric, 1878. V&A.

Blue Pomegranate wallpaper, 1866. BAL/V&A.

St James's ceiling wallpaper, 1881. BAL/V&A.

Portière, c. 1890. Designed by JH Dearle for Morris & Co. Embroidered on oak green silk damask by Mrs Battye. BAL/V&A.

African Marigold printed cotton, 1876. BAL/V&A.

Kennet woven silk, 1883. BAL/V&A.

Cabbage and Vine tapestry, 1879. BAL/V&A.

Watercolour design for **African Marigold** printed cotton, 1876. WMG.

Bachelor's Button wallpaper, 1892. BAL/V&A.

Powdered printed cotton, c. 1902. BAL/V&A.

Kennet printed cotton, 1883. V&A.

Bird and Anemone printed cotton, 1882. V&A.

Evenlode printed cotton, 1883. BAL/John Bethell.

Watercolour design for **The Orchard** tapestry, c. 1890. Designed by Morris and JH Dearle. V&A.

The Orchard tapestry, 1890. V&A.

Apple wallpaper, 1877. BAL/V&A.

Bruges wallpaper, 1888. V&A.

Watercolour design for **Wreath** woven carpet, c. 1876. WMG.

Seaweed wallpaper, 1901. Designed by JH Dearle. V&A.

Watercolour design for **Quatrefoil** rug, c. 1890. V&A.

Rose wallpaper, 1877. BAL/V&A.

Embroidered cushion cover, c. 1876. Embroidered by Catherine Holiday. WMG.

Tree portière tapestry, c. 1909. Designed by JH Dearle. BAL/Maas Gallery.

Acorn embossed or stamped silk velvet, c. 1900. V&A.

Jasmine wallpaper, 1872. BAL/V&A.

Hammersmith wool rug, c. 1880. BAL/V&A.

Wreath wallpaper, 1876. BAL/V&A.

Pen and ink design for the Kelmscott Press edition of 'Maud' by Alfred, Lord Tennyson, 1893. V&A.

Ornamental letters designed for the Kelmscott Press, 1890s. WMG.

Watercolour design for **Chrysanthemum** wallpaper, 1877. WMG.

Stained-glass window, 1878. Designed by Edward Burne-Jones and William Morris for the East window of St Denys's Church, Rotherfield. Peter Cormack.

Bullerswood carpet, c. 1889. V&A.

Larkspur printed silk, 1875. V&A.

Tile panel, 1876. Designed by Morris and made by William De Morgan. WMG.

'**16 square**' tile, 1870. Possibly designed by William De Morgan for Morris and Co. WMG.

Brocatel woven wool fabric, c. 1888. Designed by JH Dearle. V&A.

Watercolour design for **Acanthus** wallpaper, 1875. V&A.

Acanthus wallpaper, 1875. BAL/V&A.

Garden Tulip wallpaper, c. 1885. BAL/V&A.

Violet and Columbine woven fabric, 1883. V&A.

Cray printed cotton, 1884. BAL/V&A.

Daffodil printed cotton, c. 1891. Designed by JH Dearle. BAL/V&A.

Flowerpot embroidered cushion cover, 1880. WMG.

Utrecht Velvet embossed mohair plush, c. 1871. V&A.

Pimpernel wallpaper, 1876. BAL/V&A.

Watercolour design for **Avon** chintz, c. 1887. Possibly designed by JH Dearle. BAL/WMG.

Wallflower wallpaper, c. 1890. BAL/V&A.

Tile portraying Rossetti as Chaucer, 1864. Designed by Edward Burne-Jones and painted by Morris. V&A.

Carpet, 1890s. Designed by JH Dearle. BAL/Fine Art Society.

Brother Rabbit printed cotton, 1882. WMG.

Watercolour and ink design for ornamental letter for the Kelmscott Press edition of *Chaucer*, 1896. V&A.

Bower wallpaper, 1877. BAL/V&A

Grafton wallpaper, 1883. V&A.

Minstrel Angel with Dulcimer stained-glass window, 1882. Designed by William Morris for the East window of St Margaret's Church, Hopton-on-Sea. Peter Cormack

Bird woven wool fabric, 1878. BAL/V&A.

Hammersmith rug, c. 1890. V&A.

Ornamental letter designed for the Kelmscott Press, 1890s. WMG.

Eden printed cotton, c. 1905. Designed by JH Dearle. V&A.

'Praise of Venus' from *A Book of Verse*, 1870. V&A.

Design for embroidery, c. 1875. V&A.

Lodden printed cotton, 1884. V&A.

Cartoon for **The Pelican** stained-glass window, 1880. Designed for St Martin's Church, Brampton, by Edward Burne-Jones for Morris & Co. WMG.

Willow Boughs wallpaper, 1887. BAL/V&A.

Page from the Kelmscott Press edition of *Chaucer*, 1896. WMG.

Marigold printed cotton, 1875. BAL/V&A.

Fritillary wallpaper, 1885. V&A.

Woodpecker tapestry, 1885. BAL/WMG.

Watercolour design for **Rose and Thistle** printed cotton, 1881. V&A.

Artichoke embroidered hanging, 1876. Designed by Morris and worked by Mrs Godman. BAL/V&A.

Embroidered hanging, c. 1880. V&A.

Watercolour design for embroidery, 1870s. V&A.

Wandle printed cotton, 1884. V&A.

Designs for ornamental letters for Kelmscott Press books, 1890s. WMG.

Ornamental letter designed for the Kelmscott Press, 1890s. WMG.

The Strawberry Thief printed cotton, 1883. BAL/V&A.

Sunflower wallpaper, 1879. V&A.

Norwich wallpaper, c. 1889. V&A.

Tulip and Rose woven fabric, 1876. BAL/John Bethell.

Medway printed cotton, 1885. BAL/John Bethell

Watercolour design for stained-glass window, 1876. Designed for

Morris & Co for St Peter's Church, Edmgond. WMG.

Flower Garden woven silk, 1879. V&A.

Watercolour design for **Redcar** carpet, c. 1885. V&A.

Lotus embroidered hanging, 1880s. V&A.

Windrush printed cotton, 1883. V&A.

Watercolour design for cotton damask, c. 1876. V&A.

Watercolour design for **Cabbage and Vine** tapestry, 1879. V&A.

Rose printed cotton, 1883. BAL/V&A.

Ornamental letter designed for the Kelmscott Press, 1890s. WMG.

St Mary Magdalene and St John the Evangelist stained-glass window, 1865. Designed by William Morris and Ford Madox Brown for the East window of All Saints' Church, Middleton Cheney. Peter Cormack.

St Peter stained-glass
window, 1876.
Designed for St
Michael's Church,
Waterford. BAL/St
Michael's Church.

Watercolour design for
Evenlode printed
cotton, 1883. V&A.

Ispahan woven wool
fabric, c. 1888.
V&A/Daniel McGrath.

Daisy tiles, 1862.
BAL/V&A.

'Angeli Laudantes'
tapestry, 1894.
Designed by William
Morris with figures by
Burne-Jones. V&A.

Dove and Rose wool
and silk fabric, 1879.
WMG.

Honeysuckle
wallpaper, 1883.
Designed by May
Morris. BAL/V&A.

Ornamental letters
designed for the
Kelmscott Press, 1890s.
WMG.

Hornpoppy wallpaper,
1880s. Designed by
May Morris. V&A.

Wey printed cotton,
c. 1883. BAL/V&A.

Daisy wallpaper, 1862.
BAL/V&A.

Blackthorn wallpaper,
1892. BAL/V&A.

Watercolour design
for embroidery, 1870s.
V&A.

Tulip and Lily carpet,
c. 1875. BAL.

Wild Tulip wallpaper,
1884. BAL/V&A.

Anemone wallpaper,
1890s. BAL/V&A.

Ornamental letters
designed for the
Kelmscott Press, 1890s.
WMG.

Single Stem wallpaper,
1890s. Possibly by JH
Dearle. BAL/V&A.

Phaidon Press Limited
Regent's Wharf
All Saints Street
London N1 9PA

First published 1995
© Phaidon Press Limited

ISBN 0 7148 3465 3

All rights reserved. No
part of this publication
may be reproduced, stored
in a retrieval system or
transmitted in any form or
by any means, electronic,
mechanical, photocopying
or otherwise without the
prior permission of
Phaidon Press Limited.

Printed in Hong Kong

COVER: **IRIS** WALLPAPER, 1890s

TITLE PAGES: TWO DETAILS FROM **FOREST** TAPESTRY, 1887